The Young Lady\'s Equestrian Manual

The Young Lady\'s Equestrian Manual

ISBN/EAN: 9783845723112

Erscheinungsjahr: 2012

Erscheinungsort: Barsinghausen, Deutschland

www.unikum-verlag.de | info@unikum-verlag.de

Printed in Germany

Bei diesem Titel handelt es sich um den Nachdruck eines historischen, lange vergriffenen Buches. Da elektronische Druckvorlagen für diese Titel nicht existieren, musste auf alte Vorlagen zurückgegriffen werden. Hieraus zwangsläufig resultierende Qualitätsverluste bitten wir zu entschuldigen.

Covergestaltung meisterstudio ©

The Young Lady\'s Equestrian Manual

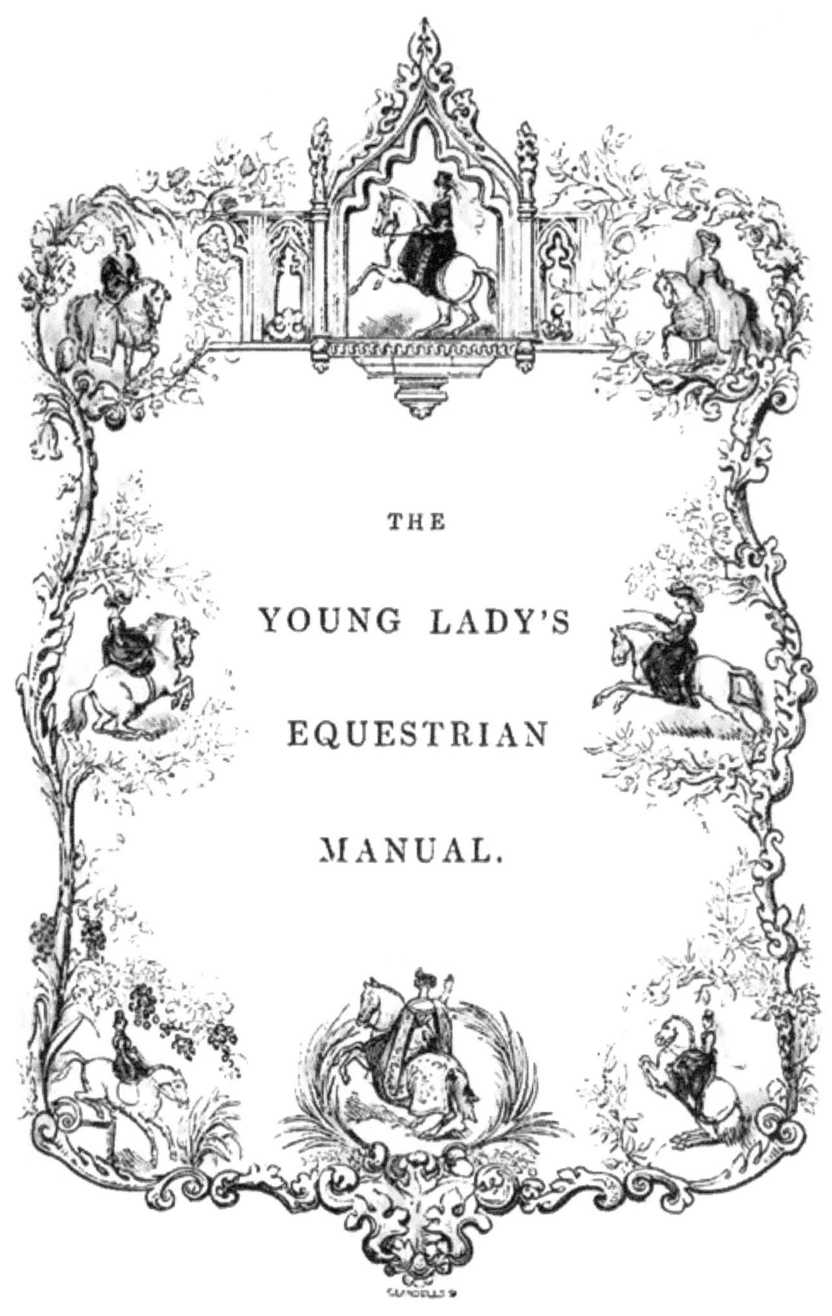

THE

YOUNG LADY'S EQUESTRIAN MANUAL.

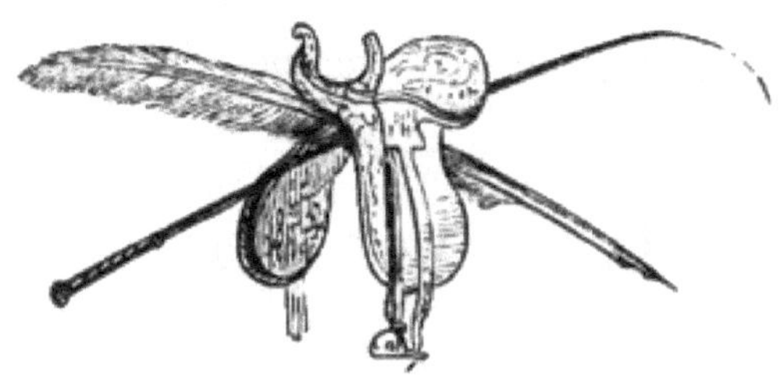

PREFACE.

THE following pages contain a Treatise on the Art of Riding on Horseback, for Ladies, which originally appeared in the Publishers' well-known Manual of elegant feminine Recreations, Exercises, and Pursuits, THE YOUNG LADY'S BOOK; with, however, various additions to the Text, and a number of new Illustrations and Embellishments.

In offering the Treatise, thus improved and adorned, in a separate form, the Publishers, it need scarcely be said, have been influenced, materially, by that high and most extensive patronage, which, under Royal auspices, has been conferred by the ladies of this country, since the commencement of the present reign, on the Art of which it is the subject.

CONTENTS.

THE

YOUNG LADY'S EQUESTRIAN MANUAL.

Our Virgin Queen, peerless Elizabeth,
With grace and dignity rode through the host:
And proudly paced that gallant steed, as though
He knew his saddle was a royal throne.

INTRODUCTION.

RIDING on Horseback is, confessedly, one of the most graceful, agreeable, and salutary of feminine recreations. No attitude, perhaps, can be regarded as more elegant than that of a lady in the modern side-saddle; nor can any exercise be deemed capable of affording more rational and innocent delight, than that of the female equestrian. Pursued in the open air, it affords a most rapid, and, at the same time, exhilarating succession of scenic changes, at a degree of personal exertion, sufficient to produce immediate pleasure, without inducing the subsequent languor of fatigue.

Nor is riding on horseback attended with that danger to ladies, attributed to it by the indolent, the melancholy, and the timid. Accidents, indeed, in the side-saddle, are of extremely rare occurrence. Strange as it may seem, it is, however, an incontrovertible fact, that horses, in general, are much more docile and temperate, with riders of the fair sex, than when mounted by men. This may be attributed, partially, to the more backward position, in the saddle, of the former than the latter; but, principally, perhaps, to their superior delicacy of hand in managing the reins.

As an active recreation, and a mode of conveyance, riding on horseback appears to have been of very remote usage among our fair countrywomen. During a long period, indeed, it was the only one known to, or, adopted by them, for the performance of journies. Such, too, appears to have been the case (with some modifications) in other European countries. The only *voiture* of the French, says Garsault, until the reign of Charles the Sixth, was the back of the horse or mule: neither Kings, Queens, Princes, nor subjects were acquainted with any other. In the time of that monarch, litters, borne by two horses, first appeared; but these were uncovered, and used, only, by ladies of the court.

Froissart describes Isabel, the second wife of Richard the Second of England, as having been borne "en une litière moult riche, qui etoit ordonnèe pour elle;" and this kind of vehicle, during the reigns of several succeeding Monarchs, appears to have been used by women of distinction in this country, but, only, it is to be observed, in cases of illness, or on occasions of ceremony. For example,—when Margaret, daughter of Henry the Seventh, went into Scotland, she generally rode "a faire palfrey;" while, after her, was conveyed "one vary riche litere, borne by two faire coursers, vary nobly drest; in the which litere the sayd Queene was borne in the intrying of the good townes, or otherwise, to her good playsher."

Towards the end of the thirteenth century, vehicles with wheels, for the use of ladies, were first introduced. They appear to have been of Italian origin, as the first notice of them is found in an account of the entry of Charles of Anjou into Naples; on which occasion, we are told, his queen rode in a *careta,* the outside and inside of which were covered with sky-blue velvet, interspersed with golden lilies. Under the Gallicised denomination of *char*, the Italian *careta*, shortly afterwards became known in France; where, so early as the year 1294, an ordinance was issued by Philip the Fair, forbidding its use to citizens' wives. Nor was England far behind in the adoption of the vehicle; for, in "The Squyr of Low Degree," a poem supposed to have been written anterior to the time of Chaucer, we find the father of a royal lady promising that she shall hunt with him, on the morrow, in "*a chare*," drawn by

> "Jennettes of Spain that ben so white,
> Trapped to the ground with velvet bright."
>
> "It shall be covered with velvet red,
> And clothes of fine gold all about your head;
> With damask white and azure blue,
> Well diapered with lilies blue."

However richly ornamented, the *careta*, *char*, or *chare*—and there is little, if any, doubt, to be entertained as to their identity—may have been, it was, probably, a clumsy, inelegant, and inconvenient structure; for its employment appears to have been far from general among high-born ladies, even on occasions of ceremony and pomp. During the fourteenth, fifteenth, and sixteenth centuries, the French Princesses usually rode on donkies; and so late as the year 1534, a sacred festival was attended by Queen Eleonora, and the females of the blood royal of France, on horseback. Nor did the superior and more recent invention of coaches, for a long period, tend materially to supersede, among ladies, the use of the saddle. These vehicles, according to Stow, became known, in England, in 1580; but, many years after, Queen Elizabeth herself is described as having appeared, almost daily, on her palfrey. In the time of Charles the Second, the fashion, among ladies, of riding on horseback, declined; during subsequent reigns, it gradually revived; and the exercise may now be regarded as firmly established, among our fair countrywomen, by the august example of their illustrious Queen.

The present graceful, secure, and appropriate style of female equestrianism is, however, materially different from that of the olden time. In by-gone days, the dame or damosel rode precisely as the knight or page. Of this, several illustrations occur in an illuminated manuscript of the fourteenth century, preserved in the Royal Library. In one of these, a lady of that

period is depicted on horseback, enjoying the pastime of the chase. In another, are represented two gentlewomen of the same period, on horseback, with an individual of the other sex, engaged (as is shewn by some parts of the design, which it would be needless, for our present purpose, to copy) in the once much-favoured diversion of Hawking.

Queen Elizabeth, says a writer in the Encyclopædia Londinensis, "seems to have been the first who set the ladies the more modest fashion of riding sideways. Considerable opposition was, at first, made to it, as inconvenient and dangerous: but, practice, in time, brought it into general use; particularly when ladies found they could ride a-hunting, take flying leaps, and gallop over cross roads and ploughed fields, without meeting with more accidents than the men: besides, it was not only allowed to be more decorous, but, in many respects, more congenial to the ease and comfort of a female rider."

Our author is, however, wrong in ascribing the fashion of riding sideways, by women in this country, to Elizabeth; by whom it could only have been confirmed, or, at the most, revived;—the honour of its introduction being clearly attributable to another Queen of England, who lived at a much more early period of our history.

Ann of Bohemia, consort of Richard the Second, is the illustrious personage to whom we allude. She, it was, according to Stow (whom Beckman follows on this point), that originally shewed the women of this country how gracefully and conveniently they might ride on horseback sideways. Another old historian, enumerating the new fashions of Richard the Second's reign, observes, "Likewise, noble ladies then used high heads and cornets, and robes with long trains, and seats, or *side-saddles*, on their horses, by the example of the respectable Queen, Ann, daughter of the King of Bohemia; who first introduced the custom into this kingdom: for, before, women of every rank rode as men do" (T. Rossii, *Hist. Re. Ang.* p. 205). In his beautiful illustrative picture of Chaucer's Canterbury Pilgrims, Stothard appears to have committed an anachronism, in placing the most conspicuous female character of his fine composition sideways on her steed. That the lady should have been depicted riding in the male fashion, might, it strikes us, have been inferred, without any historical research on the subject, from the poet's describing her as having, on her feet,

"*a paire* of spurrés sharpe."

Neither the original example of Ann of Bohemia, nor that, in later days, of Elizabeth, as female equestrians, however extensively followed, had sufficient force, entirely to abolish, among our countrywomen, the mode of riding like the other sex. In the time of Charles the Second, it appears, from a passage in the Duke of Newcastle's great work on Horsemanship, to have still, at least partially, subsisted. Another writer of the seventeenth century, whose manuscripts are preserved in the Harleian collection, speaks of it, as having been practised, in his time, by the ladies of Bury, in Suffolk, when hunting or hawking; and our venerable contemporary, Lawrence (a voluminous writer on the horse), it is worthy of remark, states, that at an early period of his own life, two young ladies of good family, then residing near Ipswich, *in the same county*, "were in the constant habit of riding about the country, in their smart doe-skins, great coats, and flapped beaver hats."

Although entirely relinquished, at present, perhaps in this country, the mode of female equestrianism under notice continues to prevail in various other localities. In the following sketch, taken from Charles Audry's magnificent "Ecole d' Equitation," a Persian lady is delineated as just about to start on a journey, in

the saddle ; and, in the next, which is engraved from an original drawing, "done from the life," a lady and gentleman of Lima are represented on horseback. "I have endeavoured," the artist says, in manuscript, on the reverse of his sketch, "to depict the horses '*pacing;*' as they are almost universally taught to do, in Peru: that is, to move both the legs, of one side, forward together. It resembles an English butcher's trot in appearance; but, it is so easy, that one might go to sleep on the horse: and, after riding 'a *pacer*,' it is difficult to sit a trotter at first. It is,

also, excessively rapid;—good *pacers* beating other horses at a gallop. The ladies of Lima do not always ride with the face covered: but, only, when the sun is powerful. They, sometimes, ride in *ponchos*, like the men: in fact, it is excessively difficult, at first sight, to determine whether a person on horseback be male or female."

The side-saddle introduced to this country by Ann of Bohemia, differed, materially, from that now used by British ladies; having, no doubt, been a mere pillion, on which the rider sate, as in a chair.

At what period our fair countrywomen first began to ride with the knee over the pommel, we are not

enabled to state: it is, however, clear, according to the original of the above sketch, which occurs in one of the historical illustrations of equestrianism, given by Audry, that the courtly dames of England did so, about the middle of the seventeenth century. Our author describes the figure, as being that of the Countess of Newcastle.

It may be conjectured, that a single crutch, only, for the advanced leg, was at first used; and this, it is not improbable, was fixed on the centre of the pommel, as in the lady's saddle, now, or at least very lately, common in some parts of Mexico; where the women, it would seem, ride with the left hand towards the animal's head. This, also, appears to have been, sometimes, the case, down to a recent period, in our own country; for, in rather a modern description of the side-saddle, the crutches are spoken of as being moveable, in order to afford a lady, by merely changing their relative positions, the means of riding, as she might please, on either side of her horse.* That a second crutch was used about the middle of the last century (we are unable to state how much earlier), in France, at least, is evident from a plate of the lady's hunting saddle, at that period, given by Garsault; in which, it is curious, a sort of hold-fast is provided for the fair equestrian's right

* Since writing the above, we have been assured by a friend, that, within a few weeks past, he has seen several ladies, at Brighton, seated on the wrong side of the horse. Side-saddles, with moveable crutches, indeed, are now far from uncommon (to our own knowledge), in saddlers' shops.

hand. But, even so recently as Garsault's time, the saddle in ordinary use, by French women, was, we learn from his work on equitation, still, a kind of pillion, on which the rider sate, diagonally, with both feet resting on a broad suspended ledge or stirrup. The pillion in this country has not yet become obsolete: being still, frequently, to be seen, on the backs of donkies and hack ponies, at watering places. During the early part of the present century, its employment continued to be general. It was fixed behind a man's saddle, on the croup of a steady horse, trained to go

at an easy though shuffling pace between a walk and a trot. The groom, or gentleman, equipped with a broad leathern belt buckled about his waist—by which the lady secured her position, in case of need—first mounted; and his fair companion was then lifted, backwards, and behind him, into her seat. In an old work on horsemanship, written by one William

Stokes, and published at Oxford, it is not, perhaps, unworthy of notice, directions are given for vaulting into the saddle, *after* the lady has been placed on the

croup; together with a plate illustrative of so exquisitely nice and marvellously absurd an operation. In Mexico

"they manage these things," if not "better," at all events, with more gallantry, than our forefathers did, for with them, "the *pisana*, or country lady," we are told, "is often seen mounted *before* her *cavaliero;* who, seated behind his fair one, supports her with his arm thrown around her waist." Our illustrative sketch of this custom (in the preceding page) is taken from a beautiful model,—the work of a native Mexican artist.

Having, now, offered our fair readers a slight and unpretending historical sketch of female equestrianism, we shall proceed, after a few preliminary remarks, to the practical details of the art.

Its various advantages, inducements, and attractions, as an exercise, have, already, been noticed. Much, however, as we wish to interest our fair countrywomen, in its favour, it is proper, on our part, to tell them, frankly, that equestrianism is far from being an intuitive art:—there is no "royal road" to it. To be enjoyed and appreciated, it must be learnt. That ease and elegance,—that comparative safety in the side-saddle, of which we have spoken,—it is impossible to achieve, without considerable practice, based upon proper principles. Many young ladies, however, feel a delicate repugnance to passing through the ordeal of a riding-school; some, again, do not reside in situations, where the benefit of a teacher's directions can be procured; while others, erroneously flatter themselves, that they are in possession of every needful acquirement, as regards equestrianism, when they have discovered how to retain a seat on the saddle, and guide a horse by means of the bridle. To such of our readers as happen to be comprised within either of these classes,—and to those, also, who, after having received a professor's initiative instructions, are desirous of further improvement, the following pages, if carefully perused, will, the writer most zealously hopes, prove beneficial.

EQUESTRIAN TECHNICALITIES.

A FEW, among the most generally adopted, of these, it will be expedient, in the first place, to notice and explain.

Most parts in the external structure of the horse are known by names of obvious signification: but such is not, exactly, the case with all.

To commence with the anterior limb:—*a* is the fore pastern; *b*, the fetlock; *c*, the leg; and *d*, the arm.

In the hind limb, *e* is the hind pastern; *f*, the hock; *g*, the stifle; and *h*, the haunch.

The upper surface of the neck, *i*, is denominated the crest; *k*, the withers, and *l*, the croup.

In the bridle, supposing it to be double-reined, *a* is the double head-stall; *b*, the front; *c*, the nose-band; *d*,

Curb Bit. Snaffle Bit.

the throat-lash; *e*, *e*, the snaffle rein; and *f*, *f*, the curb rein. At *g*, *g*, is the martingale.

In the saddle, *a*, is the *near* crutch; *b*, the off

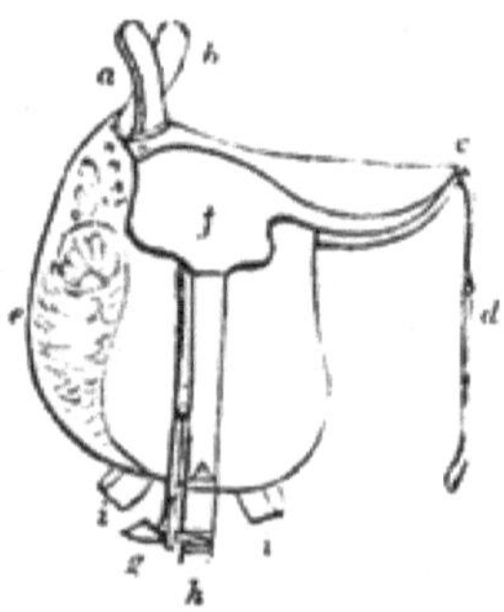

crutch; *c*, the cantle; *d*, the crupper; *e*, the safe; *f*, the skirt; *g*, the stirrup; *h*, the near side half of the surcingle; and *i*, *i*, the girths.

A lady's right hand is termed the *whip*-hand, and her left, the *bridle*-hand.

The *near* side of a horse is that which is on the *left* of the rider; and the *off* side that which is on her *right*.

The height of a horse is always estimated in *hands*, of four inches each: it is always measured at the tip of the shoulder. A horse is never spoken of as being so many hands *tall*, but so many hands *high*.

THE LADY'S HORSE.

Although the lady usually has a horse selected for her, by some gentleman, either of her own family or her acquaintance, it may not be inexpedient to inform the fair reader of those qualities which, combined in the same animal, may be said to constitute a complete lady's horse. Such a creature, however, we must observe, is exceedingly difficult to be procured, even by those possessed of the nicest judgment on the subject; and, to whom, the usually important question of price is not an object of consideration.

The beau ideal of this kind of horse is superlatively elegant in form, exquisitely fine in coat, and unexceptionably beautiful in colour; of a height, in the nicest degree appropriate to the figure of the rider; graceful, accurate, well-united, and thoroughly safe in every pace; "light as a feather" in the hand, though not at all painfully sensitive to a proper action of the bit; bold in the extreme, yet superlatively docile; free, in every respect, from what is technically denominated "vice;" excellent in temper, but still "though gentle, yet not dull;" rarely, if ever, requiring the stimulus of the whip, yet submitting temperately to its occasional suggestions.

In some, though not in all respects, the form should approach closely to that of a thorough-bred animal. The head should be small, neat, "well-set" on the neck, and gracefully "carried." The nostrils should be wide; the eyes large, rather protruding, dark, yet brilliant; the ears erect, and delicately tapering towards their tips. The expression of the countenance should be lively, animated, noble, and most highly intelligent;

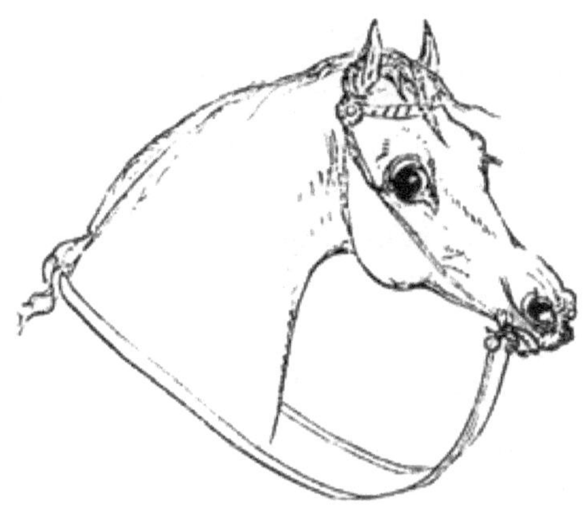

the neck rather arched and muscular; the ridge of the shoulders narrow and elevated; the chest full and fleshy; the back broad; the body, round or barrel-like; the space between the hips and tail, long, and very gradually depressed towards the latter organ, which, it is essential, should be based high on the croup. The fore and hind limbs should be distant, the one pair from the other; the "arms" muscular;

the knees broad, the hocks (laterally) wide; the legs flat and sinewy; the pasterns rather long; and the hoofs large, and nearly round.

A rough, or, what is technically termed, a "staring" coat, considerably deteriorates the appearance of a horse, however perfect in other conditions. Its surface, on a well-bred, healthy, and properly groomed animal, is not only smooth, but brilliantly polished. The mane, if too long and thick, will interfere with that delicate management of the reins so desirable to a lady on horseback; and the tail, if of immoderate length, will, by the animal's whisking it towards his sides, prove inconvenient, to the fair rider, at all times; but, especially so, in dirty weather. Neither of these appendages, however, on the other hand, should be ungracefully brief or scanty.

Of all colours presented by the horse, none is so rich, and, at the same time, so elegant and chaste, as a bright bay; provided the mane, tail, and lower parts of the legs, be black. A small white star on the forehead, and a white speck on one of the heels, are to be considered, rather, as beauties, than defects: but much white, either on the face or legs, whatever be the general hue, is quite the reverse of desirable. After bright bay, chestnut, perhaps, deserves to rank next in the scale of taste; provided it be not, as is very frequently the case, accompanied with white legs. Some of the various shades of grey, however, are, in the opinion of many, entitled to be placed above it: of these, the silver grey, with black mane and tail, claims the highest place. Brown is rather exceptionable, on account of its dulness. Black is not much admired; though, as we think, when of a deep jet, remarkably elegant. Roan, sorrel, dun, piebald, mouse, and even cream colour (however appropriate the latter may be for a state-carriage-horse) are all to be eschewed.

The height of her horse should be in harmonious proportion with that of the rider. A very young or short lady is in no less false a position, as regards grace, on a lofty steed, than a tall, full-grown woman, on a diminutive poney. For ladies of the general stature, a horse measuring from fifteen to fifteen and a half hands, at the point of the shoulder, is usually considered, as regards height, more desirable than any other.

In paces, the lady's horse should be perfect; or, at all events, so far as regards the walk and canter. The former should be fast, bold, firm, and lively, without being unsteady; and, the latter, light, easy, well-combined, and graceful: so, too, should the hand-gallop; although, it is true, a lady's horse is rarely put to this pace, unless used for the field. The trot, again, is but little practised: still the complete lady's horse is expected to be capable of performing it with great precision of step, and but little concussion to the rider:— many ladies regarding it,—however discountenanced by the majority, perhaps,—as preferable, from its vigour, liveliness, and dash, to any other pace.

To expatiate on the absolute necessity of the lady's horse being safe on his limbs, would be needless.

The mouth should be sensible of the most delicate hint of the rider's will, communicated to it by means of the bit. A horse that pulls hard, or hangs heavily upon the reins, is very unsuitable for a lady's use: so, again, is one having the mouth so tender as to suffer from moderate pressure, either by the snaffle or the curb. The former is no less fatiguing to, than the latter is distressed by, the bridle hand.

PERSONAL EQUIPMENTS.

In the selection of these, a lady has a fair opportunity for the proper display of a refined and judicious taste. All that is gaudy, needless, or even elaborate, is vulgar. Perfect simplicity, indeed, as regards, not only her own costume, but "the trappings of her palfrey," is expected, at the present day, on the part of every well-bred female equestrian.

The habit should fit the bust, without a crease: but, beneath the waist, it ought to be, not only long, but, somewhat full and flowing. Its colour should be dark as possible, without being positively black.

The hair should be plaited; or, if otherwise dressed, so arranged and secured, that it may not be blown into the rider's eyes; nor, from exercise, or the effect of humid weather, be liable to be so discomposed, as to become embarrassing.

To ride in a bonnet is far from judicious. A hat, or neat undress military cap, is indispensable to the female equestrian. It should be secured most carefully to the head: for, the loss of it would not merely be inconvenient, but, perhaps, dangerous, fròm the startling effect which its fall might produce on the sensitive temperament of the horse.

A veil is the reverse of objectionable, provided it be of moderate length, and safely tied to the hat or cap; which, it is proper to state, should have no other ornament or appendage.

The whip should be exquisitely neat and highly finished; but with little, if any, decoration.

ACCOUTREMENTS FOR THE HORSE.

Every accoutrement for the horse, however ornamental and pictorial, beyond the mere saddle and bridle, is to be rejected, as being in bad taste. The crupper and breast-band are now almost obsolete; the saddle-cloth has nearly disappeared; nettings are, generally speaking, abandoned; and the martingale itself, valuable as it may be for horses of a certain character, is rarely to be seen. Simplicity, indeed, as regards female equestrianism, is now imperatively (and, strange to say, most judiciously) enjoined, by "that same fickle goddess, Fashion," in obedience to whose sovereign behest, a lady's horse, in the olden time, was disguised, as it were, "in cloth of gold most curiously wrought."

RULES OF THE ROAD.

WITHOUT a knowledge of these, the fair equestrian, when riding in public, would be exposed to considerable inconvenience, and, often, to no slight degree of danger.

By a generally understood compact, persons, whether riding or driving, when proceeding in opposite directions, pass, each on his or her own *near*, or left-hand, side, of the road; and when on a parallel course, the faster party goes by the other, on the *off*, or right. In other words, when the former is the case, the right hands of the parties meeting, are towards each other; and, in the latter, the left hand of the faster, is towards the right hand of the slower. It follows, therefore, that when the rider is about to meet horses or carriages, she should take her ground on her *near*, or left, side of the road; and, when about to pass those travelling in the same direction with, though at a less speedy pace than, herself, on her right, or *off*. In meeting one rider, or vehicle, and, at the same time, passing, by superior speed, another, she must leave the first, on her right, and the second, on her left.

It will not be inexpedient, under the present head, to make some observations as to which side the lady should take, when riding in company with a gentleman.

Adams, a teacher of equitation, and the author of a work on the subject, remarks, that the only inducements for a gentleman to ride on the left of a lady, would be, that, by having his right hand towards her, in case of her needing assistance, he might, the more readily and efficiently, be enabled to afford it, than if he were on the opposite side; and, should any disarrangement occur in the skirt of her habit, he might screen it until remedied. On the other hand, our author observes, with great good sense, though in terms somewhat homely,—addressing, it is to be noticed, his remarks to gentlemen,—"the inconvenience of riding on the left of the lady, is, that if you ride near, to give her any assistance, you are liable to rub, or incommode, the lady's legs, and alarm her; and the spur is liable to catch, or tear, the lady's habit: if the roads are dirty, your horse, likewise, bespatters the lady's habit. On the right hand of the lady, these inconveniences do not occur, if you ride ever so close; and you are situated next the carriages, and the various objects you meet, which, in narrow roads, or, passing near, might intimidate a lady. For these reasons, I think it most proper to take the right hand of a lady."

MOUNTING.

On approaching a horse, the skirt of the habit should be gracefully gathered up, and the whip be carried in the right hand.

It is the groom's duty, when the rider approaches, to gather up the reins with his left hand, smoothly and evenly, the curb rein between, and somewhat tighter than the bridoon, properly dividing them with his fore-finger. The lady advancing, on the near side of the horse, to the saddle, receives them a little more forward than the point of the horse's shoulder, with her right hand, which still retains and passes the whip over the saddle to the *off* or right side. On taking the bridle in this manner, her fore-finger is placed between the reins: the groom then removes his hand, and the lady draws her own back, suffering the reins to glide gently and evenly through her fingers, until she reaches the near crutch of the saddle, which she takes with her

right hand, still holding the whip and reins, and places herself close to the near side of the horse, with her back almost turned towards him. The groom now quits his former post, and prepares to assist her to mount. The horse being thus left to the lady's government, it is proper, that, in passing her hand through the reins she should not have suffered them to become so loose as to prevent her, when her hand is on the crutch, from having a light, but steady bearing on the bit, and thus keeping the horse to his position during the process of mounting. She next places her left foot firmly in the right hand of the groom, or gentleman, in attendance, who stoops to receive it. The lady then puts her left hand on his right shoulder; and, straightening her left knee, bears her weight on the assistant's hand; which he gradually raises (rising, himself, at the same time) until she is seated on the saddle. During her elevation, she steadies, and even, if necessary, partly assists herself towards the saddle by her hands; one of which, it will be recollected, is placed on the crutch, and the other on her assistant's shoulder. It is important that she should keep her foot firm and her knee straight.

If these directions be well attended to, she will find herself raised to her saddle with but a trifling exertion, either, on her own part, or that of the assistant. Should

the latter be a lad only, or a groom not much accustomed to this part of his business, he should use both hands instead of one;—joining them by the fingers: indeed, this, generally speaking, is the safer mode. The lady, in all cases, should take care that her weight be well balanced on her left foot, from which she should rise as perpendicularly as possible; above all things taking care not to put her foot forward, but keeping it directly under her. The assistant should not begin to raise her until she has removed her right foot from the ground, and, by strengthening her knee, thrown her weight completely into his hand.

Having reached the saddle, while her face is still turned to the near side of the horse, and before she places her knee on the pommel, the assistant puts

the lady's left foot in the stirrup, while she removes her hand from the near to the off crutch of the saddle, holding the whip and reins as before directed.

She now raises herself on the stirrup by the aid of her right hand, while the assistant, or the lady herself, with her left hand, draws the habit forward in its place. She then places her right knee between the crutches, and her seat is taken.

Should the back part of the habit at this time, or afterwards, in the course of the ride, require any arrangement, the lady raises herself in the stirrup, by strengthening her knee, and, with her left hand, disposes her habit to her satisfaction.

THE REINS.

Pupils, during their first lessons, may arrange the reins in the following manner:—The right hand is removed from the crutch of the saddle; the reins are separated, and one is held in each hand, passing up between the third and fourth fingers, the ends being brought over the fore-fingers, and held in their places by closing the thumbs upon them, and shutting the hands: these should be on a level with each other, at a little distance apart, three inches from the body, or thereabouts, with the knuckles of the little fingers in a line with the elbow. By slightly advancing the hands, or even relaxing the hold of the reins, the horse, if well trained, will go forward. The left hand is raised to turn to the near or left side, and the right hand to turn in an opposite direction. By slightly raising and approaching both hands toward the body, the horse may be made to stop. When either rein is acted on, to turn the horse, the other should be a little slackened, or the hand which holds it relaxed.

As soon as the pupil has passed her noviciate in the art, she holds both reins in the left hand. Some ladies separate them by the third and fourth fingers; others, by one of these fingers only; and many, by the fourth and little finger: but the greater number use the latter alone for this purpose, passing the off or right rein over it, and bringing the near or left rein up beneath it. The reins are carried flat upon each other up through the hand, near the middle joint of the fore-finger, and the thumb is placed upon them so that their ends fall down in front of the knuckles. The elbow should neither be squeezed close to the side, nor thrust out into an awkward and unnatural position; but be carried easily and gracefully, at a moderate distance from the body. The thumb should be uppermost, and the hand so placed that the lower part of it be nearer the waist than the upper; the wrist should be slightly rounded, the little finger in a line with the elbow, and the nails turned towards the rider.

With the reins in this position, the lady, if she wish her horse to advance, brings her thumb towards her, until the knuckles are uppermost, and the nails over the horse's shoulder: the reins, by this simple motion, are slackened sufficiently to permit him to move forward. After he is put in motion, the rider's hand should return to the first position, gradually; or it may be slightly advanced, and the thumb turned upwards immediately.

To direct a horse to the left, let the thumb, which in the first position is uppermost, be turned to the right, the little finger to the left, and the back of the hand brought upwards. This movement is performed in a moment, and it will cause the left rein to hang slack, while the right is tightened so as to press against the horse's neck.

To direct the horse to the right, the hand should quit the first position, the nails be turned upwards, the little finger brought in towards the right, and the thumb moved to the left: the left rein will thus press the neck, while the right one is slackened.

To stop the horse, or make him back, the nails should be turned, from the first position, upwards, the knuckles be reversed, and the wrist be rounded as much as possible.

THE SEAT AND BALANCE.

The body should always be in a situation, as well to preserve the balance, as to maintain the seat.

One of the most common errors committed by ladies on horseback, who have not been properly taught to ride is hanging by the near crutch, so that, instead of being gracefully seated in the centre of the saddle, with the head in its proper situation, and the shoulders even, the body is inclined to the left, the head is brought to the right by an inelegant bend of the neck, the right shoulder is elevated, and the left depressed.

To correct or avoid these and similar faults, is important. All the rider's movements should harmonize with the paces of the animal: her position should be at once easy to herself and to her horse; and alike calculated to ensure her own safety and give her a perfect command over the animal. If she sit in a careless, ungraceful manner, the action of her horse will be the reverse of elegant. A lady seldom appears to greater advantage than when mounted on a fine horse, if her deportment be graceful, and her positions correspond with his paces and attitudes; but the reverse is the case, if, instead of acting with, and influencing the movements of the horse, she appear to be tossed to and fro, and overcome by them. She should rise, descend, advance, and stop *with*, and not *after* the animal. From this harmony of motion result ease, elegance, and the most brilliant effect. The lady should sit in such a position, that the weight of the body may rest on the centre of the saddle. One shoulder should not be advanced more than the other. Neither must she bear any weight on the stirrup, nor hang by the crutch towards the near side. She ought not to suffer herself to incline forward, but partially backward. If she bend forward, her shoulders will, most probably, be rounded, and her weight thrown too much upon the horse's withers: in addition to these disadvantages, the position will give her an air of timid *gaucherie*. Leaning a little backward, on the contrary, tends to bring the shoulders in, keeps the weight in its proper bearing, and produces an appearance of graceful confidence.

The head should be in an easy, natural position: that is, neither drooping forward nor thrown back; neither leaning to the right nor to the left. The bust should be elegantly developed, by throwing back the shoulders, advancing the chest, and bending the back part of the waist inward. The elbows should be steady, and kept in an easy, and apparently unconstrained position, near the sides. The lower part of the arm should form a right angle with the upper part, which ought to descend almost perpendicularly from the shoulder. The position of the hands, when both are occupied with the reins, or when the reins are held in one only, we have already noticed: the right arm and hand, in the latter case, may depend, easily, from the shoulder, and the whip be held in the fingers, with the lash downward, between two fingers and the thumb. The whip may also be carried in the right hand, in the manner adopted by gentlemen: the lady is not restricted to any precise rules in this respect, but may vary the position of her whip arm as she may think fit, so that she do not permit it to appear ungraceful. She must, however, take care that the whip be so carried, that its point do not tickle or irritate the flank of the horse.

The stirrup is of very little use except to support the left foot and leg, and to assist the rider to rise in the trot: generally speaking, therefore, as we have already remarked, none of the weight of the body should be thrown upon the stirrup. The left leg must not be cramped up, but assume an easy and comfortable position: it should neither be forced out, so as to render the general appearance ungraceful, and the leg itself fatigued; nor, should it be pressed close to the horse, except when used as an aid; but descend gracefully by his side, without bearing against it.

Although hanging by the left crutch of the saddle, over the near side, is not only inelegant, but objectionable in many important respects, the near crutch, properly used, is a lady's principal dependance on horseback. The right knee being passed over the near crutch, the toes being slightly depressed, and the leg pressed against the fore part of the saddle, the pommel is grasped, and the rider well secured in the possession of her seat. It is said, that when a lady, while her horse is going at a smart trot, can lean over, on the right side, far enough to see the horse's shoe, she may be supposed to have established a correct seat; which, we repeat, she should spare no pains to acquire. In some of the schools, a pupil is often directed to ride without the stirrup, and, with her arms placed behind her, while the master holds the long rein, and urges the horse to various degrees of speed, and in different directions, in order to settle her firmly and gracefully on the saddle,—to convince her that there is security without the stirrup,—and to teach her to accompany, with precision and ease, the various movements of the horse.

Nothing can be more detrimental to the grace of a lady's appearance on horseback, than a bad position: a recent author says, it is a sight that would spoil the finest landscape in the world. What can be much more ridiculous, than the appearance of a female, whose whole frame, through mal-position, seems to be the sport of every movement of the horse? If the lady be not mistress of her seat, and be unable to maintain a proper position of her limbs and body, so soon as her horse starts into a trot, she runs the risk of being tossed about on the saddle, like the Halcyon of the poets in her frail nest,—

"Floating upon the boisterous rude sea."

If the animal should canter, his fair rider's head will be jerked to and fro as "a vexed weathercock;" her drapery will be blown about, instead of falling gracefully around her; and her elbows rise and fall, or, as it were, flap up and down like the pinions of an awkward nestling endeavouring to fly. To avoid such disagreeable similes being applied to her, the young lady, who aspires to be a good rider, should, even from her first lesson in the art, strive to obtain a proper deportment on the saddle. She ought to be correct, without seeming stiff or formal: and easy, without appearing slovenly. The position we have described, subject to occasional variations, will be found, by experience, to be the most natural and graceful mode of sitting a horse:—it is easy to the rider and her steed; and enables the former to govern the actions of the latter so effectually, in all ordinary cases, as to produce that harmony of motion, which is so much and so deservedly admired.

The balance is conducive to the ease, elegance, and security of the rider:—it consists in a foreknowledge of the direction which any given motion of the horse will impart to the body, and a ready adaptation of the whole frame to the proper position, before the animal has completed his change of attitude or action;—it is that disposition of the person, in accordance with the movements of the horse, which prevents it from an undue inclination, forward or backward, to the right or to the left.

By the direction and motion of the horse's legs the balance is governed. If the animal be either standing still, or merely walking straight-forward, the body should be preserved in the simple position which we have directed the lady to assume on taking her seat. Should it be necessary to apply the whip, so as to make the animal quicken his pace, or to pull him in suddenly, the body must be prepared to accommodate itself to the animal's change of action. When going round a corner at a brisk pace, or riding in a circle, the body should lean back rather more than in the walking position: to the same extent that the horse bends inward, must the body lean in that direction. If a horse shy at any object, and either turn completely and suddenly round, or run on one side only, the body should, if possible, keep time with his movements, and adapt itself so as to turn or swerve with him; otherwise, the balance will be lost, and the rider be in danger of falling, on the side from which the animal starts. In no case, let it be remembered, should the rider endeavour to assist herself in preserving her balance, by pulling at the reins.

AIDS AND DEFENCES.

All such motions of the body, the hands, the legs, and the whip, as either indicate the rider's wishes, or, in some degree, assist the horse to fulfil them, are, in the art of riding, denominated *aids;* and those movements of the rider which tend to save the animal from disuniting himself, or running into danger, may, properly enough, be classed under the same title: while such as act for the preservation of the rider, against the attempts of the horse, when headstrong or vicious, are termed *defences.*

The aids of the hand are considered the most important: all the other actions of the rider tending, principally, to assist the bridle-hand and carry its operations into complete effect. There should be a perfect harmony in the aids; and all of them ought to be governed by those of the rein. In many instances, the power of a movement performed by the hand may be destroyed by the omission of a correct accompanying aid or defence, with the body, or the leg. Thus:—if a horse rear, it is useless for the rider to afford him a slack rein, if she do not also lean forward, in order, by throwing her weight on his fore-parts, to bring him down, and also to save herself from falling backward over his haunches. Should the rider, when her horse rises, slacken the reins, but retain her usual position on the saddle, if he rear high, she must necessarily be thrown off her balance; and then, if she hang on the bit, in order to save herself from falling, there is great danger of her pulling the horse backward.

The aids and defences of the body are numerous: we shall attempt to describe a few of them; the residue must be acquired by practice, and the lady's own observation. When the rider indicates by her hand that she wishes the horse to advance, the body should be inclined forward in a slight degree; and the left leg (with the whip, also, if the animal be sluggish, or not well trained) pressed to his side. Should she, by pulling the rein towards her, or turning the wrist in the manner we have before directed, communicate her desire to stop, her body ought, at the same time, to be thrown back, with gentleness, or otherwise, in proportion to the severity of the action of the hand against the horse's inclination to increase his speed contrary to the will of his rider, or when he leaps, kicks, or plunges. If a horse rear, the rider should lean forward more than in the aid for the advance: but care must be taken, in this case, to perform the defence with discretion, especially with a pony, or galloway; for, should the animal rise suddenly, and the rider throw herself abruptly forward, it is not improbable that he might give her a violent blow on the face with the top of his head.

We have already mentioned, in a previous part of our treatise, the direction which the body should take when riding in a circle, turning a corner, or acting as a defence against the danger attendant upon a horse's shying. In the first case, the aid of the body, if properly performed, will carry with it the aid of the hand, the leg, and even the whip, if it be held near the horse's side. We will explain this by an example:—Suppose the rider wishes to turn a corner on her left; she inclines a little towards it, drawing her left shoulder in, and thrusting her right shoulder rather forward: the bridle-hand will thus be drawn back on the near side, the off rein will consequently act on the horse's neck, and the left leg be pressed close against the near side; so that all the necessary aids for effecting her object, are performed by one natural and easy movement.

The aids of the whip, on one side, correspond with those of the leg, on the other: they are not only used in the manner we have already mentioned, when the rider wishes her horse to advance, or increase his pace, but also in clearing a corner, &c. If the lady be desirous of turning to the left, she may materially aid the operation of the hand, which directs the fore-parts of the horse to the near side, by pressing him with her stirrup leg, so as to throw his croup in some degree to the right, and thereby place it in a more proper position to follow the direction of his shoulders. In turning to the right, the whip may be made equally useful by driving out his croup to the left. The power of these aids, especially that of the whip, should be increased as circumstances require. The aid which is sufficient for some horses, may not be powerful enough by half for others: and even with the same animal, while the slightest pressure will produce the desired effect in some cases, a moderate, or, even, a rather severe, lash with the whip is necessary in others.

SOOTHINGS, ANIMATIONS, &c.

The voice and the hand, the leg, and the whole body, may be employed to soothe and encourage. High-mettled or fretful horses, it is often necessary to soothe, and timid ones to encourage. A spirited animal is frequently impatient when first mounted, or, if a horse or a carriage pass him at a quick rate; and some horses are even so ardent and animated, as to be unpleasant to ride when with others. In either of these cases, the rider should endeavour to soothe her horse, by speaking to him in a calm, gentle tone. She should suffer the whip to be as motionless as possible, and take even more than usual care that its lash do not touch the flank. Her seat should be easy, her leg still, and her bridle-hand steady. The bit should not be made to press on the horse's mouth with greater severity than is necessary to maintain the rider's command; and, as the horse gradually subsides from his animation, its bearing should be proportionately relaxed. The perfection of soothing consists in the rider's sitting so entirely still and easy, as not to add in the least to the horse's animation;—at the same time being on her guard, so as to be able to effect any of her defences in an instant, should occasion render them needful.

There is scarcely any difference between soothings and encouragements; except that, in the latter, it is advisable to *pat*, and, as it were, caress the horse with the right hand, holding the whip in the left. A shy or timid horse may often be encouraged to pass an object that alarms him, to cross a bridge, enter a gateway, or take a leap, when force and correction would only add to his fear, and, perhaps, render him incorrigibly obstinate.

Animations are intended to produce greater speed, or, to render the horse more lively and on the alert, without increasing his pace. Some animals scarcely ever require animations; while others are so dull and deficient in mettle as to call them frequently into use. The slightest movement of the body, the hand, or the leg, is enough to rouse the well-bred and thoroughly-trained animal; but it is necessary for the animations to be so spirited and united, with sluggish horses, as almost to become corrections: in fact, what is a mere animation to one horse, would be a positive correction to another.

The aids of the hand, the whip, the leg, and the body, which we have before described, are animations; so, also, are *pattings* with the hand, the tones of the voice, &c. Animations should be used in all cases, when the horse, contrary to the rider's inclination, either decreases his speed, droops his head, bears heavily and languidly on the bit, or, begins to be lazy or slovenly in the performance of his paces. A good rider foresees the necessity of an animation before the horse actually abates his speed, or loses the *ensemble* of his action, and the grace and spirit of his deportment. It is much easier to keep up, than to restore, a horse's animation: therefore, the whip, the leg, the hand, or the tongue, should do its office a few moments before, rather than at, the moment when its movements are indispensable.

A slight motion of the fingers of the bridle-hand serves as an excellent animation: it reminds the horse of his duty, awakens the sensibility of his mouth, and preserves a proper correspondence between that and the hand.

CORRECTIONS.

Ladies certainly ought not to ride horses which require extraordinary correction. For numerous reasons, which must occur to our readers, a lady should never be seen in the act of positively flogging her steed: such a sight would destroy every previous idea that had been formed of her grace or gentleness. Moderate corrections are, however, sometimes necessary; and the fair rider should make no scruple of having recourse to them when absolutely needful, but not otherwise. Astley, in his work on the management of the horse, after very properly recommending all quarrels between the steed and his rider to be avoided, observes, that too much indulgence may induce the horse to consider "that you are afraid of him;" and, our author adds, "if he should once think you are really so, you will find he will exercise every means to convince you that he considers himself your master, instead of acknowledging, by implicit obedience, that you are his."

Those, who imagine that a horse is to be corrected only with the whip, are very much mistaken. The aids and animations of the leg, the bridle-hand, the body, and the voice, may be made sufficiently severe to correct and render a horse obedient in all ordinary cases. Severe flogging seldom produces any good effect; and, in most contests between a horse and his rider, when both get out of temper, the former usually gains some important advantage. The best way to correct a horse is to dishearten, and make him do what he would fain avoid;—not so much by force and obstinate resolution, in contesting openly and directly with him, when he is perfectly prepared to resist, as, by a cool opposition and indirect means. There are different methods of attaining the same end; and those which are the least obvious to the animal should be adopted: a lady cannot rival him in physical strength, but she may conquer him by mere ingenuity, or subdue him by a calm, determined assumption of superior power.

VICES.

Some horses are addicted to a very troublesome and vicious habit of turning round suddenly,—we do not here allude to shyness, but restiveness,—without exhibiting any previous symptom of their intention. A horse soon ascertains that the left hand is weaker than the right, and, consequently, less able to oppose him; he, therefore, turns on the off side, and with such force and suddenness, that it is almost impossible, even if the rider be prepared for the attack, to prevent him.

In this case, it would be unwise to make the attempt: the rider would be foiled, and the horse become encouraged, by his success in the struggle, to make similar endeavours to have his own way, or dismount his rider. The better plan is, instead of endeavouring to prevent him from turning, with the left hand, to pull him sharply with the right, until his head has made a complete circle, and he finds, to his astonishment, that he is precisely in the place from which he started.

Should he repeat the turn, on the rider's attempting to urge him on, she should pull him round, on the same side, three or four times, and assist the power of the hand in so doing, by a smart aid of the whip, or the leg. While this is doing, she must take care to preserve her balance, by an inclination of her body to the centre of the circle described by the horse's head.

The same plan may be pursued when a horse endeavours to turn a corner, contrary to the wish of his rider; and, if he be successfully baffled, three or four times, it is most probable that he will not renew his endeavours.

On the same principle, when a horse refuses to advance, and whipping would increase his obstinacy, or make him rear, or bolt away in a different direction, it is advisable to make him walk backward, until he evinces a willingness to advance.

A runaway might, in many instances, be cured of his vice by being suffered to gallop, unchecked, and being urged forward, when he shewed an inclination to abate his speed, rather than by attempting to pull him in: but this remedy is, in most situations, dangerous, even for men; and all other means should be tried before it is resorted to by a lady. Should our fair young reader have the misfortune to be mounted on a runaway, she may avoid evil consequences, if she can contrive to retain her self-possession, and act as we are about to direct. She must endeavour to maintain her seat, at all hazards, and to preserve the best balance, or position of body, to carry her defences into operation. The least symptom of alarm, on her part, will increase the terror or determination of the horse. A dead heavy pull at the bridle will rather aid him, than otherwise, in his speed, and prevent her from having sufficient mastery over his mouth and her own hands to guide him. She must, therefore, hold the reins in such a manner as to keep the horse *together* when at the height of his pace, and to guide him from running against anything in his course; and, it is most probable that he will soon abate his speed, and gradually subside into a moderate pace. *Sawing* the mouth (that is, pulling each rein alternately) will frequently bring a horse up, in a few minutes. Slackening the reins for an instant, and then jerking them with force, may also produce a similar effect: but, if the latter mode be adopted, the rider must take care that the horse, by stopping suddenly, do not bring her on his neck, or throw her over his head.

In whatever manner the runaway be stopped, it is advisable for the lady to be on the alert, lest he should become so disunited, by the operation, as to fall.

Our readers may think, perhaps, that this advice, however easy to give, is difficult to follow: we beg leave, however, to tell them, that although it is not so easy as drawing on a glove, or replacing a stray curl, it is much more practicable than they may imagine; though, we trust, they may never have occasion to put it to the proof.

There is another situation, in which it is advisable to force the horse, apparently, to have his own way, in order to baffle his attempts. Restive horses, or even docile animals, when put out of temper, sometimes endeavour to crush their riders' legs against walls, gates, trees, posts, &c. An inexperienced lady, under such circumstances, would strive to pull the horse away; but her exertions would be unavailing: the animal would feel that he could master the opposition, and thus discovering the rider's weakness, turn it to her disadvantage on future occasions. We cannot too often repeat, that, although a rider should not desist until she have subdued her horse, she must never enter into an open, undisguised contest with him. It is useless to attack him on a point which he is resolute in defending: the assault should rather be directed to his weaker side. If he fortify himself in one place, he must proportionately diminish his powers of defence in another. He anticipates and prepares to resist any attempt to overcome him on his strong side; and his astonishment at being attacked on the other, and with success, on account of his weakness in that quarter, goes far to dishearten and subdue him. If he plant himself in a position of resistance against being forced to advance, it is a matter of very little difficulty to make him go back. If he appear to be determined not to go to the right, the rider may, on account of the mode in which he disposes his body and limbs, turn him, with great facility, to the left. If he stand *stock-still*, and will not move in any direction, his crime may be made his punishment: the rider, in such case, should sit patiently until he shew a disposition to advance, which he probably will in a very short time, when he discovers that she is not annoyed by his standing still. Nothing will subdue a horse so soon as this mode of turning his attacks against himself, and making his defences appear acts of obedience to the rider's inclination. When, therefore, a horse viciously runs on one side towards a wall, pull his head forcibly in the same direction and, if, by the aid of the leg or whip, you can drive his croup out, you may succeed in backing him completely away from it. It is by no means improbable, that when he finds that his rider is inclined to go to the wall as well as himself, he will desist. Should he not, his croup may be so turned, outward, that he cannot do his rider any mischief.

In shying, the same principle may be acted upon, more advantageously, perhaps, than in any other case. Should the lady's horse be alarmed at any object, and, instead of going up to, or passing it, turn round, the rider should manage him as we have recommended in cases where the horse turns, through restiveness. He should then be soothed and encouraged, rather than urged by correction, to approach, or pass, the object that alarms him: to attempt to force him up to it would be ridiculous and dangerous. If the horse swerve from an object, and try to pass it at a brisk rate, it is useless to pull him towards it; for, if you succeed in bringing his head on one side, his croup will be turned outward, and his legs work in an opposite direction. This resistance will increase proportionately to the exertions made by the rider. A horse, in this manner, may fly from imaginary, into real danger; for he cannot see where he is going, nor what he may run against. Pulling in the rein, therefore, on the side from which the horse shies, is improper; it should rather be slackened, and the horse's head turned away from the object which terrifies him. By this mode, a triple advantage is gained: in the first place, the horse's attention is diverted to other things; secondly,—the dreaded object loses half its terror when he finds no intention manifested on the rider's part to force him nearer to it; and, lastly,—he is enabled to see, and, consequently, avoid any danger in front, or on the other side of him.

A horse may be coaxed and encouraged to go up to the object that alarms him; and, if the rider succeed in making him approach it, a beneficial effect will be produced: the horse will discover that his fears were groundless, and be less likely to start again from any similar cause. After the first impulse of terror has subsided, the animal, if properly managed, will even manifest an inclination to approach and examine the object that alarmed him: but, while he is so doing, the rider must be on her guard; for the least movement, or timidity, on her part,—the rustling of a leaf, or the passing of a shadow,—will, in all probability, frighten him again, and he will start round more violently than before. After this, it will be exceedingly difficult to bring him up to the object. Astley, however, whom we have before quoted, says, that should the first trial prove unsuccessful, it must be repeated, until you succeed; adding, that the second attempt should not be made until the horse's fears have subsided, and his confidence returned.

A horse that is rather shy, may, in many cases, be prevented from starting, by the rider turning his head a little away from those objects, which, she knows by experience, are likely to alarm him, as well before she approaches as while she passes them.

A lady, certainly, should not ride a horse addicted to shying, stumbling, rearing, or any other vice: but she ought, nevertheless, to be prepared against the occurrence of either; for, however careful and judicious those persons, by whom her horse is selected, may be, and however long a trial she may have had of his temper and merits, she cannot be sure, when she takes the reins, that she may not have to use her defences against rearing or kicking, or be required to exercise her skill to save herself from the dangers attendant on starting or stumbling, before she dismounts. The quietest horse may exhibit symptoms of vice, even without any apparent cause, after many years of good behaviour; the best-tempered are not immaculate, nor the surest-footed infallible: it is wise, therefore, to be prepared.

Stumbling is not merely unpleasant, but dangerous. To ride a horse that is apt to trip, is like dwelling in a ruin: we cannot be comfortable if we feel that we are unsafe; and, truly, there is no safety on the back of a stumbling nag. The best advice we can offer our reader, as to such an animal, is never to ride him after his demerits are discovered : although the best horse in the world, may, we must confess, make a false step, and even break his knees.

When a horse trips, his head should be raised and supported, by elevating the hand; and the lady should instantly throw herself back, so as to relieve his shoulders from her weight. It is useless to whip a horse after stumbling (as it is, also, after shying); for, it is clear, he would not run the risk of breaking his knees, or his nose, if he could help it. If a horse be constantly punished for stumbling, the moment he has recovered from a false step, he will start forward, flurried and disunited, in fear of the whip, and not only put the rider to inconvenience, but run the risk of a repetition of his mishap, before he regains his self-possession. It being generally the practice,—and a very bad practice it is,—for riders to correct horses after having made a false step, an habitual stumbler may be easily detected. When a horse, that is tolerably safe, makes a false step, he gathers himself up, and is slightly animated for a moment or two only, or goes on as if nothing had happened; but if he be an old offender, he will remember the punishment he has repeatedly received immediately after a stumble, and dash forward in the manner we have described, expecting the usual flagellation for his misfortune.

When a horse evinces any disposition to kick, or rear, the reins should be separated, and held by both hands, in the manner we have described in a previous page. This should also be done when he attempts to run away, grows restive, or shies. The body should also be put in its proper balance for performing the defences: the shoulders should be thrown back, the waist brought forward, and the head well poised on the neck. Every part of the frame must be flexible, but perfectly ready for action.

The principal danger attendant on the horse's rearing is, that the rider may fall over the croup, and, perhaps, pull the horse backward upon her. To prevent either of these consequences, immediately that a horse rises, slacken the reins, and bend the body forward, so as to throw its weight on his shoulders; and the moment his fore-feet come to the ground,—having recovered your position, gradually, as he descends,—correct him smartly, if he will bear it; or, endeavour to pull him round two or three times, and thus divert him from his object.

The latter course may also be adopted to prevent his rearing, if the rider should foresee his intention.

A horse that displays any symptoms of kicking, should be held tight in hand. While his head is well kept up, he cannot do much mischief with his heels.

If, however, when the rider is unprepared, in spite of her exertions he should get his head down, she must endeavour, by means of the reins, to prevent the animal from throwing himself; and also, by a proper inclination of her body backward, to save herself from being thrown forward. Should an opportunity occur, she must endeavour to give him two or three sharp turns: this may also be done, with advantage, if she detect any incipient attempts in the animal to kick.

A horse inclined to rear seldom kicks much: but he may do both alternately; and the rider should be prepared against his attempts, by keeping her balance in readiness for either of the opponent defences. She must also take care, that, while she is holding her horse's head up and well in hand to keep him from kicking, she do not cause him to rear, by too great a degree of pressure on his mouth.

EXERCISES IN THE PACES.

Although our limits will not permit us to enter into an elaborate detail of the lessons taken by a pupil in the riding school, it is right that we should give the learner a few useful hints on the rudiments of riding, and not devote our whole space to the improvement of those who have made considerable progress. While we endeavour to correct bad habits in the self-taught artist,—in the pupil of a kind friend, an affectionate relative, or of a mere groom,—to confirm the regularly educated equestrian in the true principles and practice of the art,—to remind her of what she has forgotten, and to improve upon the knowledge she may have acquired,—we must not forget those among our young friends, who, having never mounted a horse, are desirous of learning how to ride with grace and propriety, and who dwell at a distance, or do not feel inclined to take lessons, from a master. To such, one-third, at least, of our preceding observations are applicable; and we recommend an attentive perusal of what we have said, as to Mounting, the Aids, &c., before they aspire to the saddle. Our other remarks they will find useful when they have acquired a little practice.

A quiet and well-trained horse, and a careful attendant, should, if possible, be procured. A horse, that knows his duty, will almost instruct his rider; and if a friend, who is accustomed to horses, or a careful servant, accompany the pupil, there is little or nothing to fear, even in the first attempts. The friend, or groom, may also, by his advice, materially assist the learner in her progress.

It would be needless for us to repeat our advice as to the manner of mounting, holding the reins, making the horse advance, stop, turn, &c., or the proper disposition of the body and limbs: all these, in her early lessons, the pupil should gradually practise.

THE WALK.

Let the pupil walk the horse forward in a straight line, and at a slow rate, supporting his head in such a manner as to make him keep time in the beats of his pace; but not holding the reins so tight as to impede the measurement of his steps, or to make him break into a trot on being slightly animated. The hand

should be so held, that it may delicately, but distinctly, feel, by the operation of the horse's mouth on the reins, every beat of his action. If he do not exert himself sufficiently, he should be somewhat animated. Should he break into a trot, he must be checked by the reins; but the pull must neither be so firm nor continued as to make him stop. The moment he obeys the rein and drops into a walk, the hand is to be relaxed. Should he require animating again, the movement for that purpose must be more gentle than before, lest he once more break into a trot.

After walking in a straight line for a short time, the lady should practise the turn to the right and to the left; alternately using both hands in these operations, in the manner directed in a previous page. She must observe, that when she pulls the right rein in order to turn the horse on that side, the other hand must be relaxed and lowered, or advanced, to slacken the left rein and ease the horse's mouth, and *vice versâ*.

If the horse do not readily obey the hand in turning, or bring forward his croup sufficiently, he must be urged to throw himself more on the bit, by an animation of the leg or whip. The animations, during the first lessons, should be commenced with great gentleness, and the rider will easily discover, by a little experience, to what degree it is necessary to increase them, in order to procure obedience. This observation should be attended to, were it only for the pupil's safety; for, if she begin with her animations above the horse's spirit, his courage will be so raised as to endanger, or, at least, alarm her, and thus render what would otherwise be an agreeable exercise, unpleasant.

After the pupil has practised walking in a straight

line, and turning on either side, for a few days, she may walk in a circle, and soon make her horse wheel, change, demi-volt, &c. The circle should be large at first; but when the pupil has acquired her proper equilibrium, &c., it must, day by day, be gradually contracted.

In riding round a circle, the inner rein is be rather lowered, and the body inclined inward. This inclination must be increased during succeeding lessons, as the circle is contracted, and the pupil quickens the pace of her horse. She must practise in the large circle, until she is able, by her hands and aids, to make the horse perform it correctly. The inside rein must be delicately acted upon; if it be jerked, at distant intervals, or borne upon, without intermission, the horse, in the former case, will swerve in and out, and, in the latter, the rider's hand, and the animal's mouth, will both become, in some degree, deadened; and thus their correspondence will be decreased. In order to procure correct action, the inner rein should be alternately borne on in a very slight degree, and relaxed the next instant,—the hand keeping exact time in its operations with the cadence of the horse's feet. The direction is to be frequently changed; the pupil alternately working to the right and the left, so as to bring both her hands into practice.

As soon as the rider becomes tolerably well confirmed in her seat and balance, and in the performance of the simple aids and animations, as well in large as small circles, she should begin to ride in double circles; at first of considerable diameter, but decreasing them, by degrees, as she improves. Riding in double circles, is guiding the horse to perform a figure of 8; and this, in the language of the riding-school, is effecting the large and narrow change, according to the size of the circles. The number of the circles may be increased, and the sizes varied, with great advantage both to the rider and the horse. They may be at some distance from each other, and the horse be guided to work from one to the other diagonally. Thus, suppose he starts from *a*, he may be made to leave the upper circle at *e*, and enter the lower one at *d*; leave it at *c*, and enter the first again at *b*; and so continue for some time: then, beginning at *f*, to quit the lower circle at *c*, enter the upper one at *b*, leave it at *e*, and enter the lower circle again at *d*. Thus, the position of the rider and horse are alternately changed, from working from the right to a straight line, thence to the left, thence to a straight line, and thence again to the right. To give an instance of riding in a greater number of circles, of different diameters, let the horse start from *a* (see figure, p. 77), and leave the upper circle at *b*, traversing to the outer small circle at *c*, passing round, so as to enter the inner circle at *e*, and going round, by *f*, to *g*; quitting it at *g*, and entering

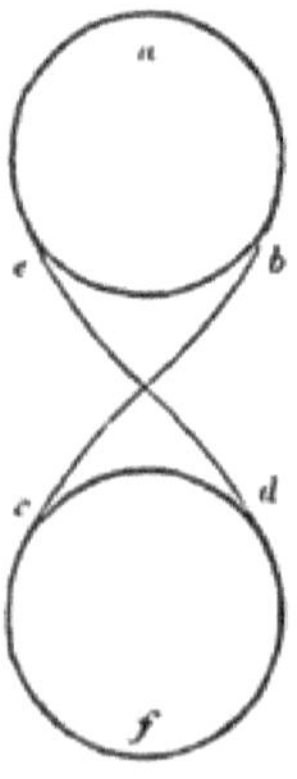

the lower circle at *h;* quitting the latter again, after passing round *i*, at *k*, and thence proceeding towards the outer small circle; entering at *l*, going round and entering the inner circle at *e*, passing round, and quitting it at *f*, to return again to *a*, by entering the upper circle at *m*. These exercises may be diversified in various ways; the pupil, for instance, may perform the upper circle, and one or both of the pair below, return to the upper circle, cross from that, diagonally, to the lower circle, quit it, at *h* or *k*, to perform one of the middle circles, return to the lower circle again, pass thence to the other middle circle, and quit it at *c* or *f* (as the case may happen), to return to the upper circle again. Nothing can be more beneficial than this variety of action; it tends at once to confirm the pupil in her seat; to exercise her in her balance and aids; and to render the horse obedient: while, if he be kept in only one direction, he will perform the figure mechanically, without either improving his own mouth and action, or the rider's hands, aids, or balance.

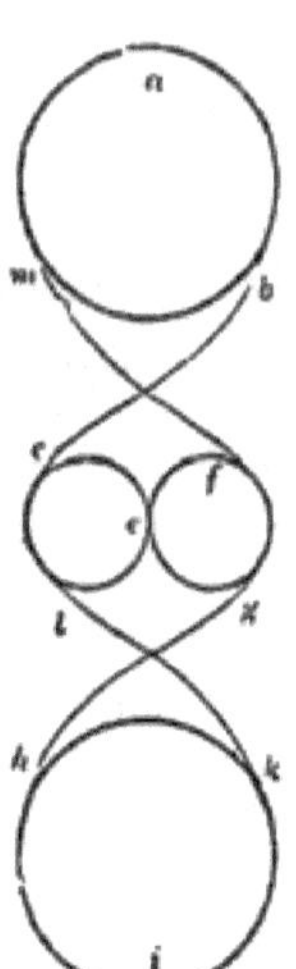

In the art of riding, working on a circle is called a *volt;* in angles, or a zig-zag direction, *changes reverse;* and on half a circle from a line, a *demi-volt*. These figures may first be performed separately; but there can be no objection to the demi-volt and changes reverse being afterwards embodied in the exercises on circles. As in the last figure, the lady may work from *a* in the mode directed, for some time; then perform the variations, by going across from *a* to *b*, and describe a demi-volt round by *c e* to *a;* then return from

14

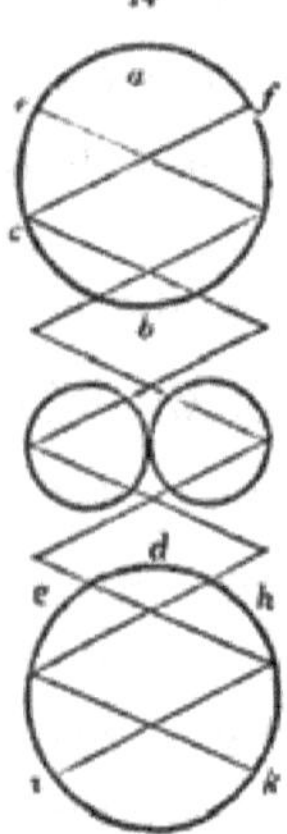

a to *b*, and work a demi-volt, in an opposite direction, from *b* to *a:* thence, the lady may proceed in a line, enter the lower circle at *d*, and re-commence riding in circles. The change reverse may at any time be performed, by quitting the upper circle at *e* or *f*, and working on the traversing lines, so as to cross the lower circle at *g* or *h*, and enter it at *i* or *k*. In fact, these exercises may be varied, *ad libitum;* and the more they are diversified, the greater advantage the lady will derive from them, provided she persevere until she can perform one figure with accuracy, before she enter upon another that is more complicated. Should the horse, in changing, yield his head, but withhold his croup so as to destroy the union of his action, or mar the perfection of the change, the rider should bring it to the proper position, or sequence, by an aid of the whip or leg, as the case may be.

THE TROT.

The lady should begin to practise this pace as soon as she is tolerably perfect in the walking lessons. It will be as well for her, at first, to trot in a straight line: she may then work in the large circle, and proceed, gradually, through most of the figures which she

has performed in a walk. To make the horse advance from a walk to a trot, draw upwards the little finger of each hand (or that of the left hand only, when the pupil has advanced enough to hold the reins in one hand), and turn them towards the body: an animation of the leg or whip should accompany this motion. The trot should be commenced moderately: if the horse start off too rapidly, or increase the pace beyond the rider's inclination, she must check him by closing the hands firmly; and, if that will not suffice, by drawing the little fingers upwards and towards the body. This must not be done by a jerk, but delicately and gradually; and, as soon as the proper effect is produced, the reins are again to be slackened. If the horse do not advance with sufficient speed, or do not bring up his haunches well, the animations used at starting him are to be repeated. When the horse proceeds to the trot, the lady must endeavour to preserve her balance, steadiness and pliancy, as in the walk. The rise in trotting is to be acquired by practice. When the horse, in his action, raises the rider from her seat, she should advance her body, and rest a considerable portion of her weight on the right knee; by means of which, and by bearing the left foot on the stirrup, she may return to her former position without being jerked; the right knee and the left foot, used in the same manner, will also aid her in the rise. Particular attention must be paid to the general position of the body while trotting: in this pace, ordinary riders frequently rise to the left, which is a very bad practice, and must positively be avoided. The lady should also take care not to raise herself too high; the closer she maintains her seat, consistently with her own comfort, the better.

THE CANTER.

THE whole of the exercises on circles should next be performed in a canter; which may be commenced from a short but animated trot, a walk, or even a stop. If the horse be well trained, a slight pressure of the whip

and leg, and an elevation of the horse's head, by means of the reins, will make him strike into a canter. Should he misunderstand, or disobey these indications of the rider's will, by merely increasing his walk or trot, or going into the trot from a walk, as the case may be, he is to be pressed forward on the bit by an increased animation of the leg and whip;—the reins, at the same time, being held more firmly, in order to restrain him from advancing too rapidly to bring

F

his haunches well under him; for the support of which, in this position, he will keep both his hind feet for a moment on the ground, while he commences the canter by raising his fore feet together.

The canter is by far the most elegant and agreeable of all the paces, when properly performed by the horse and rider: its perfection consists in its union and animation, rather than its speed. It is usual with learners who practise without a master, to begin the canter previously to the trot; but we are supported by good authority in recommending, that the lady should first practise the trot, as it is certainly much better calculated to strengthen and confirm her in the balance, seat &c. than the canter.

The lady is advised, at this stage of her progress, to practise the paces, alternately, in the various combinations of the figures we have described; performing her aids with greater power and accuracy in turning and working in circles, when trotting or cantering, than when walking. She should also perfect herself in her aids, the correspondence, and balance, by alternately increasing and diminishing the speed in each pace, until she attain a perfect mastery over herself and her horse, and can not only make him work in what direction, and at what pace, but, also, at what degree of speed in each pace, she pleases.

The horse ought to lead with the right foot: should he strike off with the left, the rider must either check him to a walk, and then make him commence the canter again, or induce him to advance the proper leg by acting on the near rein, pressing his side with the left leg, and touching his right shoulder with the whip. His hind legs should follow the direction of the fore legs, otherwise the pace will be untrue, disunited, and unpleasant, both to horse and rider: therefore, if the horse lead with his near fore leg (unless when cantering to the left—the only case when the near legs should be advanced), or with his near hind leg, except in the case just mentioned—although he may lead with the proper fore leg—the pace is false, and ought to be rectified.

THE GALLOP.

No lady of taste ever gallops on the road. Into this pace, the lady's horse is never urged, or permitted to break, except in the field: and not above one among a thousand of our fair readers, it may be surmised, is likely to be endowed with sufficient ambition and boldness, to attempt "the following of hounds." Any remarks, on our part, with regard to this pace, would, therefore, be all but needless.

STOPPING AND BACKING.

The lady must learn how to perform the perfect stop in all the paces. The perfect stop in the walk, is a cessation of all action in the animal, produced instantaneously by the rider, without any previous intimation being given by her to the horse. The

slovenly stop is gradual and uncertain. The incorrect stop is a momentary and violent check on the action in the middle, instead of the conclusion, of the cadence, while the fore legs are coming to the ground. The proper movements should be performed, by the rider, so that the stop may conclude correctly with the cadence. The firmness of the hand should be increased, the body be thrown back, the reins drawn to the body, and the horse's haunches pressed forward by the leg and whip, so that he may be brought to bear on the bit.

The stop in the trot is performed as in the walk: the rider should operate when the advanced limbs of the animal, before and behind, respectively, have come to the ground, so that the stop may be perfected when the other fore leg and hind leg advance and complete the cadence.

The stop in the canter is performed by the rider in a similar manner: the time should be at the instant when the horse's fore feet are descending;—the hind feet will immediately follow, and at once conclude the cadence. In an extended canter, it is advisable to reduce the horse to a short trot, prior to stopping him, or to perform the stop by a *double arrêt;*—that is, in two cadences instead of one.

It is necessary that the lady should learn how to make a horse *back*, in walking: to do this, the reins must be drawn equally and steadily towards the body, and the croup of the horse kept in a proper direction by means of the leg and whip.

LEAPING.

In riding-schools, ladies who never intend to hunt, are frequently taught to leap the bar. The practice is certainly beneficial; as it tends to confirm the seat, and enables the rider more effectually to preserve her balance, should she ever be mounted on an unsteady or vicious horse.

Leaps are taken, either standing or *flying*, over a bar, which is so contrived as to fall, when touched by the horse's feet, if he do not clear it: it is placed at a short distance from the ground, at first; and raised, by degrees, as the rider improves. The standing leap, which is practised first, the horse takes from the halt, close to the bar. The flying leap is taken from any pace, and is easier than the standing leap, although the

latter is considered the safer of the two to begin with; as, from the steadiness with which it is made by a trained horse, the master or assistant can aid the pupil at the slightest appearance of danger.

The position of the rider is to be governed in this, as in all other cases, by the action of the horse. No weight is to be borne on the stirrup; for, in fact, pressure on the stirrup will tend to raise the body, rather than keep it close to the saddle. The legs—particularly the right one—must be pressed closely against the saddle, and the reins yielded to the horse, so that the rider can just distinguish a slight correspondence between her own hand and the horse's mouth. The animations thus produced, and the invitation thus given, will make the horse rise. As his fore quarters ascend, the lady is to advance forward; the back being bent inward, and the head kept upright and steady. A moment before the horse's hind legs quit the ground, the body should be inclined backward; the rider taking care not to bear heavily on the reins, lest the horse force her hand, and pull her forward on his neck, or over his head, as he descends. When the leap is cleared, the rider should bring the horse together, if at all disunited, and resume her usual position.

In the flying leap, the seat is to be preserved as in the standing leap; except, that it is needless, and, indeed, unwise, to advance the body as the horse rises: because, in the flying leap, the horse's position, especially in a low leap, is more horizontal than when he rises at the bar from a halt; and there is great danger of the rider being thrown, if she lean forward, in case the horse suddenly check himself and refuse the leap; which circumstance occasionally happens. The waist should be brought forward, and the body suffered to take that inclination backward which will be produced by the spring forward of the horse. The horse's head is to be guided towards the bar, and the reins yielded to him as he advances.

The proper distance for a horse to run previous to the leap, is from ten to fifteen yards. If he be well trained, he may be suffered to take his own pace; but it is necessary to animate an indolent animal into a short, collected gallop, and urge him, by strong aids, to make the leap.

DISMOUNTING.

The first operation, preparatory to dismounting, is to bring the horse to an easy, yet perfect, stop. If the lady be light and dexterous, she may dismount without assistance, from a middle-sized horse: but, it is better not to do so if the animal be high.

The right hand of the lady, when preparing to dismount, is to receive the reins, and be carried to the off crutch of the saddle. The reins should be held sufficiently tight to restrain the horse from advancing; and yet not so firm as to cause him to back or rear; nor uneven, lest it make him swerve.

The lady should next disengage her right leg, clearing the dress as she raises her knee; remove her right hand to the near crutch; and then take her foot from the stirrup.

Thus far the process is the same whether the lady dismount with or without assistance.

If the lady be assisted, the gentleman, or groom, may either lift her completely off the saddle to the ground; or, taking her left hand in his left hand, place his right hand on her waist, and, as she springs off, support her in her descent. She may also alight, if she be tolerably active, by placing her right hand in that of the gentleman (who, in this case, must stand at the horse's shoulder), and descend without any other support. Should there be any objection to, or

difficulty found in alighting by either of these modes, the gentleman, or groom, may place himself immediately in front of the lady, who is then to incline sufficiently forward for him to receive her weight, by placing his hands under her arms, and thus easing her descent.

If the lady dismount without assistance, after the hand is carried from the off to the near crutch, she must turn round so as to be able to take, in her left hand, a lock of the horse's mane; by the aid of which, and by bearing her right hand on the crutch, she may alight without difficulty. In dismounting thus, without assistance, she must turn as she quits the saddle, so as to descend with her face towards the horse's side.

By whatever mode the lady dismounts, but especially if she do so without assistance, she should—to prevent any unpleasant shock on reaching the ground—bend her knees, suffer her body to be perfectly pliant, and alight on her toes, or the middle of her feet. She is neither to relinquish her hold, nor is the gentleman, or groom, if she make use of his ministry, to withdraw his hand, until she is perfectly safe on the ground.

In order to dismount with grace and facility, more practice is required than that of merely descending from the saddle after an exercise or a ride. It is advisable to mount and dismount, for some days, several times, successively, either before or after the ride;—commencing with the most simple modes, until a sufficient degree of confidence and experience is acquired to perform either of these operations in a proper manner, with the mere aid of the assistant's hand.

CONCLUDING REMARKS.

THE lady should perform her first lessons with a snaffle bridle, holding the reins in both hands, and without a stirrup. When she has acquired some degree of practice in the balance, aids, and general government of the horse, she may use a bridle with double reins, and hold them in the left hand, managing them as we have directed in some of the preceding pages.

If the lady be but in her noviciate in the art, we strongly advise her not to place too much reliance on her own expertness, or to attempt too much at first; but, rather, to proceed steadily, and be satisfied with a gradual improvement; as it is utterly impossible to acquire perfection in the nicer operations of riding, before the minor difficulties are overcome.

The lady, in all cases, should recollect that her horse requires occasional haltings and relaxation. The time occupied in each lesson should be in proportion to the pace and animation in which it has been performed. If the exercise be varied and highly animated, the horse should rest to recruit himself at the expiration of twelve or fifteen minutes; when refreshed, by halting, he may be made to go through another of the same, or rather less duration, and then be put up for the day. It would be still better to make two halts in the same space of time;—the exercise taken in such a lesson being equal to three hours' moderate work. When the lessons are less animated, they may be made proportionally longer; but, it is always better, if the pupil err in this respect, to do so on the side of brevity, than, by making her lessons too long, to harass her horse.

Zeitfracht Medien GmbH
Ferdinand-Jühlke-Straße 7
99095 Erfurt, Deutschland
produktsicherheit@kolibri360.de